One
Amazing Day
with Papa

Fredrich William Jensen

Published by
Hasmark Publishing
www.hasmarkpublishing.com

Permission should be addressed in writing to Fredrich William Jensen at Fredrichsbooks@gmail.com

Cover & Book Layout: Anne Karklins
anne@hasmarkpublishing.com

Illustrations: Matrix Media Solutions (P) Ltd.
www.matrixnmedia.com

ISBN 13: 978-1-989161-74-6
ISBN 10: 198916174X

Hasmark
PUBLISHING

Dedicated to William Henry Jensen
The world's greatest Papa! He was Awesome!!
10/19/1940 –12/04/2018

One awesome day I find myself fishing with my Papa. It was the best day I ever had!

My mom, sister and Nana were there too.

It was a bright and sunny day.

First my Papa taught me how to put the bait on the fishing hook.

Then my Papa helped me catch a fish.
It was so exciting to be
catching a fish and to be with my Papa.

We had to release the fish
because it was too small.

My Papa also helped my sister
but she didn't catch a fish.

My sister and I took a break and then got chased by a cranky goose.

Once we were all done we came home and I got to tell my Daddy all about my amazing day with Papa.

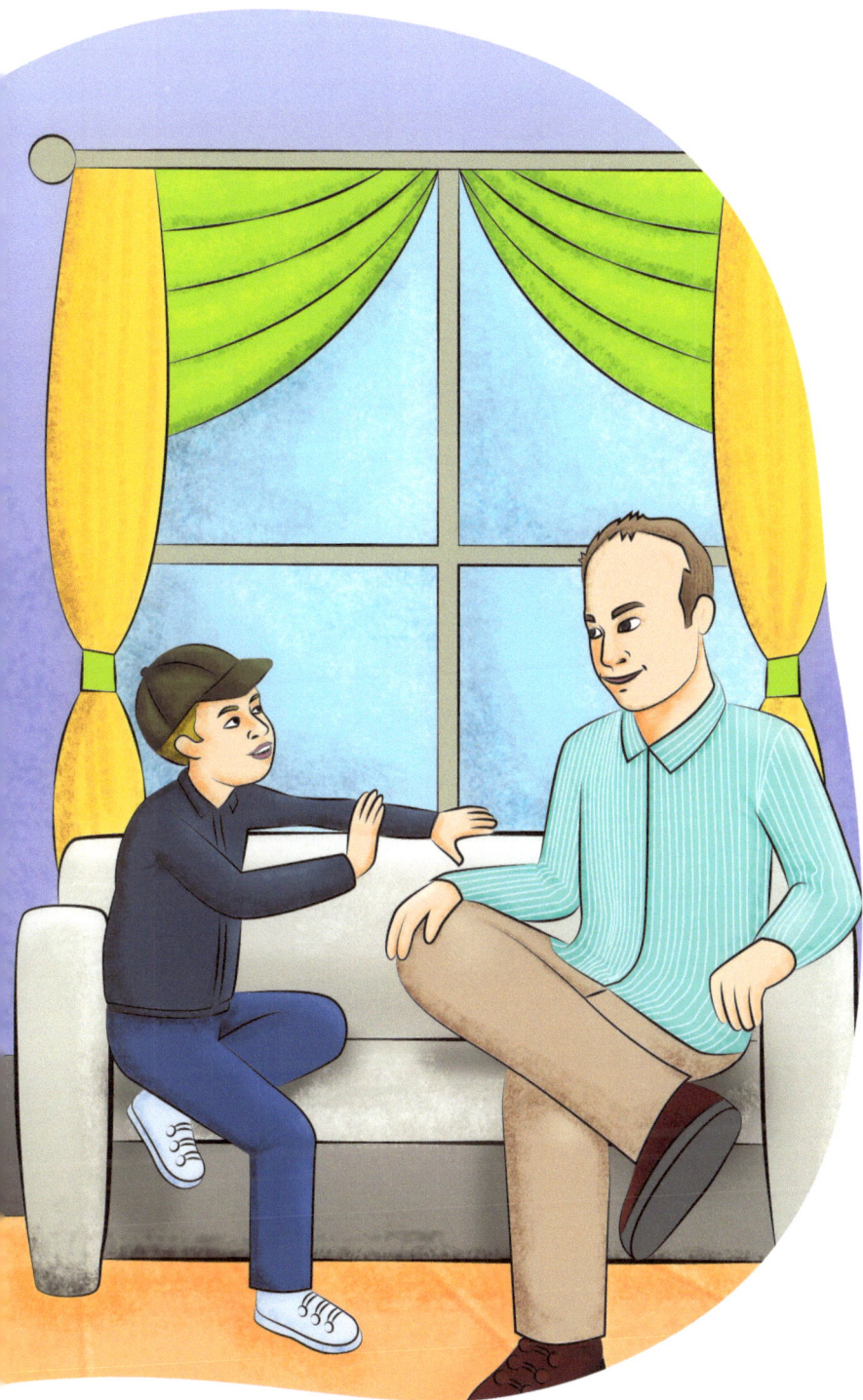

My family and me.

About the Author

Fredrich William Jensen is an avid reader and outdoor enthusiast. When not writing, he is participating in little league baseball, Cub Scouts, or out playing with friends. He is finishing his second grade year of school where his educators have been a terrific influence to help lead the way toward this book and many others to come.

www.ingramcontent.com/pod-product-compliance
Lightning Source LLC
Chambersburg PA
CBHW041523090426
42737CB00037B/23